Narcissism
&
Co-Dependency

From the series...
"At the Chalkface of Therapy"

Published in 2015 by FeedARead.com Publishing – Arts Council funded

ABOUT MICHAEL ACTON-COLES

B.Ed., M.Ed. (Psych.) Hons., M.A. C.Psych., P.D. C.Psych.

Michael Acton-Coles has over two decades of clinical and counselling experience with individuals, couples and families.

Born in England and educated in Eire and England, he started his career in psychology early and between the ages of 13 and 16 worked for one day a week in the children's ward of a psychiatric hospital, an extra-curricular activity with his school that was originally meant to be for just six months. As well as providing him with a bus pass and a free meal, this sent Michael on a journey of self-discovery. After contracting meningitis at 16 and nearly dying, he left home at 17 and went on to become a teacher; his first teaching post was in a prison in Kent.

Travelling became a strong element in Michael's life – Saudi Arabia, the UAE, Bahrain, the USA, France and Australia gave him teaching contracts which enabled him to complete his Master's degree with psychological honours; at 27 he became a Graduate Member of the British Psychological Society.

Michael's first clinical job was at the Dundee Royal Infirmary where he worked for two years in a Chronic Pain Outpatients' Department. During this time he was held at gunpoint while walking home and held for a number of hours. Facing death, his listening skills and prayers eventually secured his release.

This experience changed him: he suffered from PTSD and became involved with a psychotherapist who introduced him to working in a psychodynamic way.

Michael left Dundee and moved to Sussex to work and research alongside Dr Mick Burton and Professor Mic Cooper on psychodynamic therapy. After two years he achieved his Master's in Counselling Psychology and worked within the NHS at both the outpatients' psychology department and drug dependency unit; he also counselled patients with HIV and AIDS, for charitable organisations.

At 35, Michael applied for a Doctorate in Counselling Psychology at London City University – one of thousands of applicants for 23 places. Not expecting to get a place, he also applied to complete a Family Law degree and was accepted into the top three law colleges in the UK. But he did receive a letter offering him a place at London City University and was also asked, by The London Institute, to set up a private practice in their London Clinic. This was due to his work background in substance abuse, identity issues, life crisis and gender dysphoria; his work and research into chronic pain and disability and also his work with the issues reported by people who identify themselves as lesbian, gay, bisexual or transgendered.

In 2004 he took a sabbatical to work and travel in America and Australia where he researched suicide prevalence and prevention.

Throughout Michael's life journey he has studied many philosophical areas and has an interest in philanthropy, Shamanism and philosophy.

Narcissism
&
Co-Dependency

Both Sides of the Coin

Michael Acton-Coles

"Being a codependent is like having high blood pressure. It can be a silent killer..." – Michael Acton-Coles

CONTENTS

I NO LONGER...

"I no longer have patience for certain things, not because I've become arrogant, but simply because I reached a point in my life where I do not want to waste more time with what displeases me or hurts me. I have no patience for cynicism, excessive criticism and demands of any nature. I lost the will to please those who do not like me, to love those who do not love me and to smile at those who do not want to smile at me.

*I no longer spend a single minute on those who lie or want to manipulate. I decided not to coexist anymore with pretense, hypocrisy, dishonesty and cheap praise. I do not tolerate selective erudition nor academic arrogance. I do not adjust either to popular gossiping. I hate conflict and comparisons. I believe in a world of opposites and that's why I avoid people with rigid and inflexible personalities. In friendship I dislike the lack of loyalty and betrayal. I do not get along with those who do not know how to give a compliment or a word of encouragement. Exaggerations bore me and I have difficulty accepting those who do not like animals. And on top of everything I have no patience for anyone who does not deserve my patience." - **Meryl Streep**

This quote was chosen because it encapsulates the goal and attitude that all codependents need to aim for as part of their healing; thank you Meryl.

ACKNOWLEDGEMENTS

Firstly, I wish to thank Neil Hocking, an amazingly loyal colleague and friend who manages to wear so many hats and helps me to achieve.

Secondly, to Raili Ahlroos for her invaluable publishing experience and helpful input on matters of formatting and language.

Next, to friends, family and loved ones, and to all those that have been part of my personal and professional journey and given me experiences (both helpful and not so good): I have learned from you all with a thirst and gratitude.

Without my daughter Victoria, I would not have had the motivation and determination to provide, be a good example and to burn the midnight oil. Every hug, snuggle and kiss made it all seem worthwhile. And now my beautiful grandchildren, Taylor and Lewis, inspire me to help people help their future and the world they are stepping into.

And finally, to every patient's soul that has come to me for help over all this time of practising: by inviting me into your world and working with me you have taught me so much. You have taught me more than I could have ever imagined possible. I thank each and every one of you for this unimaginable reward and gift. It has, in turn, helped us help so many.

AUTHOR'S NOTE

Many books dealing with NPD (Narcissistic Personality Disorder) focus solely on the narcissist and the pathological traits that lie behind his or her behaviour; less attention is paid to the other side of the coin, the codependent.

To understand the basic pattern of the narcissist-codependent relationship, think of the two individuals as dancers at an evening party. The narcissist is the perfect lead on the dance floor: confident, self-assured and decisive. He (or she) engages with everyone, asking each in turn to dance, yet none of the dance partners they take quite match up. Perhaps they misread the narcissist's movements and step on his or her toes, or are too rigid to just lie back and enjoy being swept away in the moment. Finally, the narcissist approaches the humble codependent who has been watching all along, as if mesmerised, from the shadows. A moment later and the narcissist is asking the codependent to dance. The codependent, amazed at their luck, accepts the invitation and, within minutes, the two are gracefully sweeping around the room. The acquiescent codependent watches their partner's every step with the care and attention they have grown up learning to provide. The pair adapt and move perfectly together and the dance seems effortless and a joy to watch. The narcissist laps up the attention from his partner and those who are watching in awe.

The codependent, carried away by the drama and romance of it all, believes that they have met the partner of their dreams and waits for the day when the narcissist looks back at them, eyes brimming with mutual respect and love – but that moment never comes.

They try ever harder to prove their worth as a dance partner, yet the narcissist barely recognises the effort, wrapped up as they are with how they appear to others around them. As bitterness grows and self-esteem crumbles, the codependent looks across the dance floor for options but sees no-one looking back; fear paralyses them. They realise they will never find someone as eligible as the narcissist and so must choose between being alone in the shadows of life or continuing in a dance that no longer holds any enjoyment for them bar the glimmers of hope that keep them there ('who would ever love me?') The narcissist has now completely taken control, reaffirming the codependent's childhood fears of not being lovable. The key to the codependent is their self-destructive belief that they are responsible for their significant others' happiness or misery. They lack the ability at this point to separate out and see the whole 'damned' picture. This is the moment when they become trapped – unless they can find a path to healing the wounds that lie behind their maladaptive behaviour.

There is hope for peace and happiness, but if you are reading this book or if you know somebody this book will help, the codependent is already in the grip of distorted thinking.

It is my sincere hope that this book compiled through years of scholastic and evidence-based therapeutic practice enables the suffering codependent to realise their predicament and to take their first steps upon that healing road. In recognition that few readers will be seasoned academics, I have deliberately kept my language plain and concise, and let the case examples do much of the talking. This focus on readability, accessibility and economy is a seam that runs through the '*At the Chalkface of Therapy,*' series of books.

Thank you for reading.
Michael Acton-Coles

FOREWORD

This '*At the Chalkface of Therapy*' series of books, of which *Narcissism: Both Sides of the Coin* is the first, was born from Michael's strong desire to find a way to make constructive use of his twenty-plus years of working with patients at the chalk face of therapeutic psychological intervention. He had considered returning to an academic faculty and applying his experience in a research-based model. However, after many discussions with friends and family, he realised that he did not want to be tied down to academic convention or to have his ability to travel between the USA and UK hindered by being responsible to a university.

So he decided instead on a more conducive option: to write accessible and comprehensible books on certain clinical areas that he works in, books that cover the definitions and academic opinions you would expect from a psychological text but that also contain 'human' examples to help provide a more effective understanding.

In organising this book, Michael has tried to ensure the content is balanced, taking note of current research and evidence-based practice whilst illustrating what happens in the real world with real patients in real therapeutic settings.

Throughout this book, the reader will follow the journey of a couple, John and Jackie, whose experiences and interactions, inside and outside of the therapy room, illustrate the dynamic talked about in the main text. Whilst John and Jackie are real people, their names and other details about them have been changed, as have some of the specific experiences discussed. This is to protect their identities while remaining true to the gist of their experiences.

For ease of reading, these clinical examples are highlighted in ***bold italics*** throughout the text and preceded by a picture of Michael.

Michael's motivation and reward in writing this series of books is partly a revisitation of his educative years and partly an opportunity for him to present and promote psychiatric, therapeutic and psychological evidence alongside all that he has learned from those he describes as his, "hard-working and humbling patients."

The result is a very powerful mix which should help the reader and/or their friends and family members to dispel myths, clarify where they are in their own lives and to ultimately make sound decisions about their safety, wellbeing and future.

Michael says: "If this book helps just one person then I have been extremely successful in my endeavour. And I want to know; so please see the **Links & Further Information** section at the back of the book to find out how you can give useful feedback so that I can continuously learn and review."

Throughout his time as a therapist, Michaels' mantra has been to help those who would ordinarily struggle to access professional therapy. In keeping with this, Michael has consistently provided financial assistance for around 25% of his patients.

PART 1: UNDERSTANDING NARCISSISM & CODEPENDENCY

1. DEFINING NARCISSISM

Introduction

Personality disorders are a controversial area within psychology, so much so that wholesale revisions were made to their treatment in the psychiatrists' 'bible' – the DSM-5 (Diagnostic and Statistical Manual version 5) – when the fifth edition was released in 2013. So it is not surprising that there is a lot of misinformation – or at least one-sided information – out there on Narcissistic Personality Disorder (NPD). Much of the published information, in books and articles, originates from victims of narcissists and while their voices most certainly need to be heard, their judgment is usually impaired by their own closeness to the situation.

Specifically, they are likely to ignore or downplay their own role in co-creating the environment in which a narcissist can flourish – and this is not surprising given that victims of NPD are so used to being ignored themselves.

In a strange way, the characteristics of the narcissist and their victim are mirrored in the DSM-5 itself: NPD was on the verge of being eliminated from the DSM-5 altogether but refused to relinquish its entitlement to separate diagnosis.

On the other hand, whilst most psychologists would agree that narcissists can only thrive in a codependent relationship, the codependent partner is usually identified by association, perhaps referred to as an 'inverted' or 'reverse' narcissist, or the provider of 'narcissistic supply.'

To me my rooms often feel like cavernous wells, where people pour in their pitchers of ideas, stories and viewpoints along with their many assorted feelings, thoughts and aspirations. Everyone in life has their very own stories and, clearly, no one completely escapes the ruggedness of their time on this planet. From desperation to enlightenment, our journeys take us down many pathways.

I often have people present to me who identify narcissistic traits in their partner, parent or child and, at times, even worry that they see these qualities in themselves. Truth is, we all have narcissistic traits; it's part of being human and also one of our most necessary defences against harm. Think about it: when we catch a miserable cold, study for an exam, prepare for a special meal or even work on the garden after a hard winter we must focus and give our all to that project – at that time. Nothing exists for us apart from our own needs and wants (unless of course an emergency should arise). 'Our' world is all that matters and we need the rest of the world to understand that 'we', and what's immediately at hand for 'us', come first and everyone else needs to agree on its importance and support us. When we are in depression or illness we focus on ourselves, our issues and our needs; we often burn out friends and people close to us because we drone on and on about our loss, our difficulties, our struggles and our blame.

It is normal and healthy to be egocentric at times – all about 'me, me, me' – but if we don't have NPD we get that this cannot go on and, sooner or later, we restore a balance between our own needs and those of others. However, someone with NPD will feel that this attention is, and always will be, their given right and, underneath their mask, will feel no emotion towards the plight of another. Nevertheless, they are capable of sending all the right signals to those outside their familial context and have a well-rehearsed ability to charm, say the right things and to generally be the 'belle of the ball'.

When I publish articles on certain aspects of narcissism, what generally follows is a swift spike in referrals/enquiries from people who are really suffering from the impact of such unhealthy relationships. These people, in immense pain, will identify with much of what I write about narcissism. Now, this need not be about their partner: it can also be about a significant other such as their own child, grandchild or parent, or a close friend. Narcissism, and narcissistic traits, knows no boundaries and narcissists may impact any and all who are close to them. I can work with narcissists on their problematic traits to a degree: NPD is an attitude that has developed from early childhood and I can help them in their attempt to manage it in order to improve life for them and their significant others. But in my experience, narcissism is not something we, as therapists, can eradicate in our therapy rooms.

If you are reading this and feel that you are being hurt by a person with NPD, the only elements that you can change relate to you and your circumstances, and I am hopeful that just this one remark will enable you to start thinking seriously about this.

To be in a significant relationship with someone with NPD is a very confined and extremely lonely place, and, as a codependent, you need to know that it is fear and need that are keeping you safe in this familiar dance or dynamic – but fear and need will not keep you happy, content or emotionally safe in the long run.

Narcissism in Psychiatry

NPD is one of ten specified Personality Disorders in the DSM-5 main manual. According to the manual: "Personality disorders are associated with ways of thinking and feeling about oneself and others that significantly and adversely affect how an individual functions in many aspects of life."[1]

Although the APA (American Psychiatric Association) have considered replacing the long-standing categorical model of personality disorders with a controversial trait-based system, this approach has so far proven too complex and so the categories remain for now. However, NPD does also form one of six types of Personality Disorder in the trait-based system, which has been included as a separate section (Section III). However, it should be understood that there is no clear dividing line between where one 'flavour' of personality disorder ends and another starts.

Nevertheless, the further categorisation of Personality Disorders into clusters helps to refine diagnosis somewhat, with NPD one of four "Cluster B" mental disorders, the so-called, "Dramatic, emotional, erratic cluster," where it sits alongside Antisocial Personality Disorder (ASPD), Histrionic Personality Disorder (HPD) and Borderline Personality Disorder (BPD).

---

1   Personality Disorders factsheet, www.dsm5.org, published
    2013, last accessed 17/11/2014

As with all of the personality disorders in the DSM-5, NPD is characterised by both an impairment of personality and unhealthy traits.

Specifically, narcissists:

! Draw their identity and self-esteem from others. They use others to hold up an inflated or deflated opinion of themselves. This self-appraisal can fluctuate between the two poles with emotions swinging up and down in response.
! Set goals based on their (often unrecognised) need for approval. Their standards are either impossibly high or, conversely, appallingly low (since they feel entitled to special treatment so feel no need to make any effort).

In relationships, narcissists:

! Have little empathy with the needs and feelings of others.
! Take notice of others' reactions only if it directly affects them.
! Have limited awareness of the effects of their actions on others.
! Are only superficially involved, using intimacy as a way to regulate self-esteem.

The pathological traits of NPD are:

! Antagonism, due to an exaggerated self-importance and an overt or hidden sense of entitlement (grandiosity). This can cross over into violence and 'narcissistic rage' if their self-esteem is wounded.
! Attention-seeking, with a need to be admired by others.

As mentioned in the introduction, everyone is narcissistic to a degree, although popular books from the last decade (e.g. *'Generation Me'* and *'The Narcissism Epidemic'*) point the finger particularly at those born in the 1980s and 1990s.

However, any psychiatric diagnosis of NPD requires symptoms that go beyond what is expected from the person's stage of development, their socio-cultural background and the temporary effects of any legal or illegal drugs.

So what does the narcissism-codependent dynamic look like at the chalkface?

It was early Spring, with just an edge of bitterness in the wind commingled with the freshness of the sun which streaked across Earls Court Square as I walked to my rooms, familiar and comforting to me after my having practised there for 15 years. I picked up my regular coffee to welcoming smiles from the familiar people at the local coffee house; I habitually weighted down my coffee with nutmeg, cinnamon and three Sweet 'N Lows. The mixed spice aroma was warming; it was a perfect moment to start preparing for my day.

I crossed the street, opened the iron gate and descended the cold, hard stairs to the big blue entrance door. My first new intake of the day was clearly following close behind for, as soon as I set down my coffee and began to get out my files and various accoutrements for the day, the door buzzer went. Now patients are asked to be no more than ten minutes early, so as to help protect the identity of those patients finishing their sessions and also to help minimise interruptions, but this intake was 35 minutes early!

Some people travel significant distances at times, even using long-haul flights, so I usually suggest that they use my local coffee shop to gather themselves before arriving; but today a man and a much younger woman were already standing there and shuffling slightly, so I welcomed them in, asked them to take a seat and said that I would be with them at 10.00, their allotted time.

I returned to my room and continued my ritual of setting up for the day. I have used the same, now straggly, clipboard for many years. It displays the emblem of one of my first universities and still serves me well as a hard surface on which to write my session notes. Every day is new; my work is never dull. I never know what to expect from the individuals, couples and families I work with, particularly with new intakes.

I walked into reception and into an atmosphere that could have been cut with a knife but my new couple both rose, with beaming smiles and outstretched hands, and introduced themselves. From their accents I concluded that they were not from London, although they were very polished and well heeled. And charming. Charming always rings early warning bells for me; most people are anxious and, if anything, a little humble coming to see me (it goes with the stigma of seeing a shrink, let's be honest!)

So when people are overconfident, approaching me as if they were at a charity cocktail party or entering into a high brow business meeting, I wonder where their emotions and feelings are at. Pleasant is one thing, but over-the-top, engineered introductions become immediately interesting to me. They scream about well-defended souls; is it because of fragility or terror? Are they self-serving or compliant? Masquerading or keeping the peace? Who is who and what is what?

My mind always goes into top gear because the first meeting gives valuable information, introducing me to initial clues about what we will be working with together; and they are usually clues to issues and traits the people cannot see for themselves. Most people presenting to me report that they have wound up in their dysfunctional and harmful position in life unknowingly, as if it crept up on them. They "had no idea," and "can't fathom it!" They "would NEVER have guessed!"

How about when it comes to the pathological traits of NPD or codependency (CD)? No one would usually question or look behind the charming façade of an NPD-CD dance. There are few clues. In fact, so well-rehearsed and fabulous is that dance that neither the perpetrator nor the victim themselves have a clue what's going on. But while the NPD-CD dance is the causation, the symptomatology is what really presents as painful and terrifying. Do these symptoms ring any bells: loneliness in the relationship; feeling small, not respected, ridiculed, invisible, physically abused, financially abused, emotionally abused, hooked-in and unable to move, misunderstood, unhealthy or anxious; experiencing Obsessive-compulsive Disorder (OCD); feeling deskilled, forlorn, inadequate or always wrong?

The locking in of the CD to the NPD is so complete, and has (usually) been comfortable for so long, that patients present with the symptoms above rather than bringing up a specific NPD-CD problem.

In particular, seeing oneself as someone with NPD appears to be very difficult in my rooms. In fact I have never, in over 20 years of practice, had someone with NPD presenting for help. Codependents are usually so exhausted that they just cannot see that they are part of the dance; their most urgent need is to free themselves from all of the hooks and traps that have been set for them, but acknowledging their role as a codependent is a huge part of the healing process.

NPD Statistics

How many narcissists are out there? According to psychiatrists, 1% of people satisfy the diagnosis for NPD, with men making up three out of four cases. But the narcissist's lack of self-awareness makes it highly likely that this figure is a gross underestimate.

It is very important for me to add here that these statistics have also not sufficiently explored the same-sex and transgendered population and rely heavily on incomplete research. I have seen extreme examples of NPD in same-sex couples and in the transgendered population over the years. While I have not found the occurrence disproportionately high or low when comparing its prevalence with that in people that identify as heterosexual, the fact that there is no mention of diversity at all in the official stats indicates that the figures may not be a complete or accurate picture.

Since psychologists, psychotherapists and GPs are generally the first point of call for NPD symptomatology, people such as myself, working at the chalk face, will certainly find NPD much more prevalent than these stats suggest and understand that it is not gender specific. In my experience NPD knows no boundaries and can be present in any person regardless of class, gender, age, nationality or social context.

As I've already touched on, most psychiatrists and therapists will tell you that narcissists are among the hardest patients to work with and are unlikely to ever seek help for themselves.

If circumstances do bring them to the clinic they will often treat the professionals with contempt and leave after one or two sessions at most.

Back to our early arrivals left sitting in the waiting room. My opening expression, to bring patients into the room and encourage them to engage, is: "So what brought you to be in this room with me today?" I leave a purposeful silence in order to allow myself time to observe and consider the body language, eye contact and other features of the emerging dynamic.

As I am figuring out who's who in this relationship dance, I am also giving them the space to 'bring themselves.'

At the outset I was caught from far left field as John struck viciously with an outpouring of contempt for me. He didn't mess around. He then went on, in a more pleasant manner, to explain that it was Jackie with all of the issues and that he would do anything he could to help her and her situation. He complained about how she had changed of late (they had been together for seven years) and that she no longer knew what she was doing. He explained how Jackie was getting increasingly distraught and cried stupidly with no reason. I asked for an example of this:

Recently, in the build-up to Christmas, John and Jackie had been at a supermarket. John described Jackie's panic attack at the checkout, reporting that she had been tight-chested, unable to breathe and crying inconsolably. At this point, Jackie moved from her hunched and frail posture and took up a forward-leaning purposeful stance. She was looking at John from underneath a black cloud of despair – a cloud latent with irritation. It seemed a well-practiced position. She looked as if she were exploding inside but diverting an outburst by shaking her leg violently and chewing her lips; but her eyes … they were fierce, at once pleading and full of rage towards John. My heart was pounding but I kept calm and remained accepting, open and inquisitive.

Throughout, John glanced at Jackie several times but seemed to not register her twisted and tormented being. As he was coming to the end of his quite thorough commentary of Jackie's emotional volatility I asked him to observe Jackie and consider what was taking place with her. Was it similar to how she was at the supermarket checkout? He affirmed that it was.

I enquired of Jackie: "Jackie, thank you for allowing John to speak; now tell me what is going on for you right now." It was as if a tap had been instantly turned on. Jackie looked to the floor, then pleadingly towards John and I and then back to John and finally back to the floor. There was a box of tissues set on the table, equidistant between John and Jackie for easy reach. Jackie did not reach for tissues and John did not offer. John looked at Jackie and then looked away, and then looked at me and with a shrug said: "See what I mean?"

As a practitioner I hold back on comforting a patient in distress as I wish to help them engage with the discomfort and understand it as it is happening rather than extinguish the flames; this helps us to find a pathway back to the cause of distress and upset, often hidden so deeply the patient doesn't comprehend it. But how did John react? Jackie's partner of seven years seemed to show no concern or empathy and ridiculed her plight. It seemed he felt that Jackie was causing unrest and that <u>he</u> was the victim. Could John have an undiagnosed position? Why doesn't Jackie just leave this man? Hmmm?

We will return to John and Jackie later.

Narcissists are NOT in Love with Themselves

"Life is a stage, and when the curtain falls upon an act, it is finished and forgotten. The emptiness of such a life is beyond imagination" - **Alexander Lowen**

It is often incorrectly stated that people with NPD are in love with themselves, but nothing could be further from the truth. Looking more closely at the disorder, narcissists are out of touch with their real selves and this "self" that they admire – and even adore – so much is nothing more than a fake construct, a mask behind which they can hide the terrible shame and self-loathing they feel within. Of course, hiding away behind a false mask is not peculiar to narcissists. But men and women with NPD have found a way to use their masks to steal the energy they are unable to source for themselves from others. They are so skilled at creating this mask that they often come across as confident and charming; but this is only the handsome, well-dressed facade behind which the vampire lurks.

Far from being in love with themselves, narcissists feel chronically empty and unloved, constantly haunted by the fear of being discovered for the wretched fakes they are and the unbearable shame which that would cause them.

To defend themselves, they expend lots of energy controlling their appearance, behaviour and environment to extract maximum admiration by 'proving' their superiority over others. This is what is meant by the term 'grandiosity,' one element of the antagonistic personality trait described in the DSM-5.

But once the narcissist feels they are losing the floor, the mask slips and either the petulant child or the intimidating bully is likely to make an appearance. This is one of the telltale signs of the narcissist.

Jackie, having spent a good two minutes sobbing and taking shallow, sharp breaths, finally growled through clenched teeth at John. She explained in more detail the supermarket experience: "We were at the checkout and John was told that one of the special offer vouchers had expired the day before. John tried to charm the checkout girl, explaining that, as a regular customer, he must have, upon this occasion, made an oversight. The checkout girl explained that the discounts were automatically deducted by the computer and there was nothing she could do. At the same time, people in the queue behind were making comments as our shopping was backing up. John turned from charming and smooth to rage. Red-faced and pushing me out of the way, he started to carelessly shove the shopping into bags. I reminded him that we needed to be careful as there were a few delicate gifts in one of the bags. John shushed me out of the way and continued to ram items in, stomping like a child – but a scary child. I felt invisible, not heard, insignificant, disrespected, not cared for – so many feelings. After years and years of this I felt I was going to explode. I just couldn't move. I pleaded with John. Once the shopping was loaded into the trolley John was polite again, thanked the check-in girl, pulled me away by my arm and told me to stop making a scene."

Are Narcissists Born or Made?

There is no one clear cause of NPD, but a history of trauma, including verbal abuse has been put forward as a strong risk factor. Conversely, an indulgent family background, where the parents shielded the child from disappointment by pandering to their every need, has been put forward as another. However, the fact that narcissists can exist among non-narcissistic siblings demonstrates that parenting alone is unlikely to be the sole cause. For the same reason, genetics cannot be the sole determinant, although various studies have provided evidence for at least an element of genetic predisposition; for example, narcissists may be afflicted with a nervous response system that is hypersensitive to external stimuli. Combine these risk factors with a 'Western' society where individualism, competition and the creation of glamour are encouraged and you have the ideal conditions in which narcissists can flourish. In a sense, society itself has yet to develop to the stage where creating an authentic self, and learning to be comfortable with it, is the norm rather than an exception.

So let's now look at John's family background and current circumstances. Even at their young age, John and Jackie live in a multi-million dollar property in a city centre with no mortgage. John was brought up by parents who were quite religious.

His father had been very successful and Mum was a stay-at-home mum, with a perfectionist personality, who kept everything in order. John struggled with his PhD completion and was also put on psychiatric drugs at this time. Nevertheless, he quickly rose to the top of his field in science and also secured a substantial income from a second job. The couple report that John has a well-adjusted and successful sister with her own family, who is very loving and caring and has been married for over a decade. John feels pressure to always be the best and is very competitive with his sister towards whom he feels great resentment. In session, John is defensive and volatile when challenged.

The problem with constructing a false ego and disowning the less palatable parts of the psyche is that people end up projecting their inner conflict without and creating mayhem in the world around them. In essence, this is exactly what narcissists do.

According to John, Jackie is the hysterical part of this relationship and he is the calm and collected, successful and patient partner.

In order to keep up appearances – to themselves and others – narcissists will eventually resort to using the weapons of fear and pain, controlling those closest to them and keeping them from abandoning the relationship; this is their worst nightmare.

Narcissists latch on to the belief that 'survival of the fittest' is the end game of existence and that any show of weakness makes them vulnerable to attack. This sets up a winner versus loser dynamic with narcissists determined to place themselves in the former category.

They, and to some extent society at large, have failed to understand that maintaining healthy boundaries while being authentic is where real strength and the desire to do good come from.

John presents Jackie as the self-obsessed 'ungrateful victim,' a clear case of a person with NPD projecting himself upon his codependent victim! Of course, if this happens daily, weekly, monthly – then the codependent's own insecurities are being deeply and dangerously affirmed.

As mentioned before, NPD transcends gender, race, religion, sexual orientation and socio-economic class, but some (inconclusive) studies have highlighted differences in its manifestation. For example, in heterosexual relationships male narcissists tend to show the more overtly violent, controlling aspects of the disorder, perhaps helped or 'enabled' in this because women are more biologically and psychologically inclined to stay longer in an abusive relationship than is healthy. Under this supposition, women tend to be more focused on fixing 'the one' relationship rather than looking for other opportunities, and this is intensified if she also has a *passive dependent* personality type, an old-fashioned psychiatric label for those who tend to become *codependents*.

As of 2015, no reputable research exists that details the dynamics of NPD in same-sex couples or any variability regarding narcissistic or codependent traits in people who identify as Lesbian, Gay, Bisexual, Transgender, Queer (LBGTQ).

However, in my practice I have come across no differences in the prevalence or manifestation of NPD in same-sex couples or where people with gender dysphoria (GD) are involved. This is an area of research which is neglected and could add valuable understanding to this NPD phenomenon.

"You must not hate those who do harmful things; but with compassion, you must do what you can to stop them – for they are harming themselves, as well as those who suffer from their actions." – Dalai Lama XIV

2. ENTER THE CODEPENDENT

I feel so small.
I am pushed down all the time.
Self-esteem drained.
Nothing left of me.
Don't believe the nice things anymore.
I'm bad.
Nothing if I'm not with... .
Who would ever want me?
I'm unloveable.
Feel so much shame.
I'm not important.
Terrified to be alone.
So stuck.
Double bind: damned if do; damned if don't.
People don't believe me.
Don't know what happened.
Well, in the beginning I was adored.
Nobody wants me.
Can't seem to do anything right.
I feel I am nothing.
I see others in love.
So different when we are alone.
Feel discarded.
Others are worse off.
Can't do anything right.
I'm stupid and selfish.
I feel nothing.

These are the most common utterances I hear from patients who are victims of living with a person with NPD.

The term codependency came into common usage when addiction groups such as Alcoholics Anonymous realised that addicts were often enabled in their harmful behaviours by their partners and other family members. Just like the addicts themselves, their partners exhibited denial and deceitful behaviour to ensure they retained control over their own positions in the relationships – that of irreplaceable caregivers. The extent of the abusive behaviour *codependents* would tolerate, towards themselves and others, was observed to go far beyond what most people would agree was healthy.

But codependency is not restricted to substance addictions, and is often observed in the relationships of those with certain personality disorders, especially the Cluster B disorders such as BPD and, of course, NPD. In fact, codependency is *required* for narcissists to have close relationships at all and, unfortunately, they are adept at seeking out and luring *codependents* into their lives. They are so fearful of being alone with their despised selves that their quests for a partner become obsessions which can easily masquerade as passionate love.

Although there is no specific psychiatric definition of codependency, denying it the scrutiny of other pathologies, therapists are very much aware of the early life experiences that end up with people taking on that role. For example, children who grow up in homes where addiction or abuse is ongoing – or where one or more of the caregivers are themselves narcissists – are particularly vulnerable to forming codependent relationships in the future. In childhood, their survival and emotional wellbeing will have been so wrapped up in attending to the needs of others that their own identities will have become dependent on playing the role of the martyr. Having known only 'transactional' or conditional love, they have rarely, if ever, experienced the joy of being loved for who they are.

Jackie is a university professor and the daughter of blue-collared workers in Ireland. She has a strict Catholic background with a passive father and dominant mother. Mother was 42 (and an immigrant) and Father was 54 when they had Jackie. Jackie was the first in her family to go to University; she became the 'perfect child,' angelic in every way with polite manners and the grades she needed to achieve. Growing up, she was not abused in the true sense of the word but she quickly learned that she only received approval, kindness and her mother's love when she was exceptional and faultless. So Jackie became a pleaser to her mother and never really figured out her own needs and wants. Mother had NPD and fed off Jackie's achievements, boasting about her daughter to everyone in her village. Therefore, Mother only looked as good as Jackie did. When Jackie did not do so well, or stepped off the princess perch for a moment, she was quickly punished with silence, looks of disapproval and the withdrawal of love and affection. Consequently, she developed anxiety and attachment issues and became very lonely and isolated. Jackie developed into a star codependent: "Mother loves me when I do everything she needs. If Mother's world is OK then mine will be OK and I will be loved.'

Just like narcissists, *codependents* feed off the approval of others but, in their case, they define their self-worth by how well they provide for their partners. Sadly, all efforts to serve narcissists are futile as they cannot recognise nor appreciate the *codependents'* efforts.

Jackie: "It was a Friday and we had both had a busy week at work. I put some flowers out, baked John's favourite cake and spruced myself up. John didn't acknowledge me; he walked right past me and the flowers, and though I could see he saw the cake, he went straight into the office. I went after him and explained what I had done. He said it was lovely but he had important things to finish and he would be with me later. I cried and he screamed at me for always making it 'about me' and said that he was tired of me ruining his evenings. He explained the importance of his job, that he was tired, had just got in from work and that he hadn't time for any of this. I just felt that there was nothing I could do to make him feel special, that I never got it right and that I should be more understanding and not bother him. I always seem to get in the way somehow. I'm not like this at work, only at home with John. It seems I can fool people at work but when people get close to me they see the real me and it's not worthy; I just can't seem to get it right. Another ruined night and another night alone. John is busy and I must understand this."

In essence, an *NPD-codependent* dynamic is a marriage made in Hell: two people locked together in a dance of mutual need, one compelled to please, the other compelled to seek admiration. Neither can exist without the other, yet true love and companionship eludes them both.

There is similarity here with domestic abuse situations because many, if not all, abusers are narcissists and their victims are filling the only remaining role in a codependent relationship. Again, it needs to be made clear that both men and women suffer with NPD and that same-sex relationships are equally at risk of entering into this unhealthy dynamic.

Why Codependents Make the Perfect Match

Socialised to serve, the *codependent's* childhood need for a mother or father figure to appease is shifted on to their partner. They mistake their own desperation to please, based on a fear of rejection, for love. Just like the narcissist, the *codependent* has no resources for dealing with being alone.

To recover, a *codependent* desperately needs to work on defining what belongs to them and what belongs to others (i.e. creating boundaries). But, trapped in a relationship with a narcissist, that becomes impossible since the narcissist is constantly working against that aim, to erode what few boundaries the *codependent* does have so that they will tolerate a far greater level of abuse than is healthy. This is rarely understood by those who are outside and looking in.

Jackie explained that she has slowly eroded away and disintegrated into the relationship, losing herself in the process. The relationship had started with her being swept off her feet and paraded in front of John's friends, colleagues and family as smart, beautiful, amazing and special. John apparently idolised and loved Jackie and she was so happy because she had found her true love. He was such a catch too: charming, tall, handsome, wealthy, accomplished and well-respected by everyone.

But at home, once Jackie was hooked into the familiar pattern of her relationship with her mother, she slowly and surely began to replicate it with John.

Because she adored and loved him, she would become aware of the clues that she was trained to pick up on: that something wasn't quite right or that she needed to take care of him better (because John was 'much more important than her').

Even when John's abusive and disrespectful behaviour became obvious and too much to bear she felt she had no choice; she had nothing else. Everything was in his name, since he earned so much more than she, and she had signed a postnup. If she left she would have only a suitcase. She was a failure as a daughter and who would want her after failing this relationship too?

Jackie has had amazing career success and is respected for her academic achievements. She has some close friends and is very attractive and well put together. But she feels worthless and 'in the way' – a waste of space – without John. John also believes Jackie has nothing without him and that he is all she needs and all she should want. In his mind, Jackie is fortunate that he puts up with her at all, even though she could damage his reputation and image if she does not continue to do everything right (in his way, in his time).

Jackie has been working so hard at not upsetting John and being there to assist him, that she has neglected friends and family and isolated herself; John is really becoming all she has.

Any affection, attention and commitment that is showered on the narcissist never reaches past the image. No matter what the *codependent* does, the narcissist will eventually move the goalposts or raise the bar to ensure they fail. And as the narcissist abuses this failed self that they are projecting on to their victim, the *codependent*, in turn, recognises their own lack of self-love and accepts their lot.

It is a slow and gradual but very definite progression and a difficult phenomenon to step back from and understand. Friends and family rarely suspect a thing as all seems charming, perfect and ideal.

3. EARLY SIGNS: RECOGNISING & AVOIDING THE NARCISSIST

Chaos and Destruction

Narcissists are not only largely oblivious to the pain and suffering they cause to those connected with them, they actually perceive their own lack of emotional intelligence as more evidence in support of their unique qualities, as a strength which lifts them above those around them. Tragically, *codependents* recognise their narcissists' insecurities and put their whole beings into trying to 'fix' them. As they strive to do better and to be more worthwhile partners, parents or children, the narcissists take the opportunity to offload all of their self-hate onto their willing victims over which they begin to assert complete dominance and maintain their pathological illusion of power.

This has tragic consequences, with the tormented partners ending up more psychologically damaged the longer they stay in the situation. Their only recourse is to escape the relationship and to seek therapy to help them to fully disconnect and work towards recovery. The impact of narcissists' abuse on those they are in a close relationship with should not be underestimated as it affects everything that the personality is founded upon.

Very few people who have walked the corridors of my therapy rooms this past few decades have stayed with a partner with NPD. They have often worked like dogs to adapt, change themselves and accept their partner's traits but, in the end, it is usually a question of life and death. The only two people I know to have continued in their relationship to date were those who stepped back, recognised the situation, made a life for themselves separate from their relationship and expected very little from their partner. Both had multiple affairs but they stayed together for practical reasons, played the narcissist's required game and were fulfilled outside of the relationship. Both are in the public eye and "for now" it serves them well to stay together.

In the early stages of a relationship, the person with NPD is highly skilled at presenting themselves as level-headed, caring, generous and considerate. They are often so focused on obtaining the narcissistic supply that only an intimate relationship can provide, that they are frighteningly skilled at quickly and powerfully sourcing a romantic partner.

The victim/*codependent* falls for the mask, unaware of the danger he or she is heading for, particularly the young and naïve who have not had the life experience or parental guidance that can save them. The more wary might pick up on the narcissist's Achilles' Heel – their insatiable need to be admired; if the attention isn't on them, the narcissist will quickly show signs of boredom, frustration and even anger.

For many others, the dream begins to unravel gradually with the narcissist subtly increasing their power at the expense of their partner's. By the time any overt physical or psychological coercion begins, the *codependent* is already deeply enmeshed in the relationship: a web of destruction.

Unable to form a genuine loving bond, the narcissist will also destroy parents, children and even work colleagues in his or her campaign for ultimate control.

Jackie and John approached me for couples work. John stayed for two sessions and told me that he felt I was qualified, exceptionally experienced and really good at my job. He praised me and told me confidently that I was the person that could help his Jackie, because, to him, it was Jackie who desperately needed my help.

After working with Jackie for a few individual sessions we came to engaging in this dialogue: "Jackie, we have been working for a while now and I sense you are lost; it is very difficult to see <u>you</u> in the stories you are telling me. Might I pull us both back and review where we are? You have spoken about you mother, your siblings, your colleagues and John; however, through all of this I really do not know what you are here to accomplish. I feel it would be an idea to think about what Jackie needs, what Jackie wants."
There was a very long silence; Jackie looked at the floor directly in front of her feet. I kept quite still and silent and had to remind myself to breathe for I felt I had knocked the nail of the issue on the head. Slowly Jackie raised her head and with a soft but assertive and reflective delivery she said: "What an unusual and interesting question. What's more interesting is I really don't know. My initial thought was to have John and I happy again but I realise 'want' and 'need' are very different. I need John to be happy again, but what do I want? What does Jackie want? How can I know what I want when I don't even know who I am. I DON'T KNOW WHO I AM." Jackie released a haunting howling moan. Her face contorted and she visibly deflated in front of my very eyes. Jackie had made a 'shift.'

In psychological terms she had seen her reflection and no one was there.

Jackie had been serving mother and John her entire life; John had simply replaced her mother. She discovered that even her choice of academic degree was made to please her mother. The place where she lived with John was not her choice of home; she lived there because he liked it. She realised that there was not one picture on the wall that she had chosen or even liked; in fact, when she had expressed liking something John had talked her out of getting it. All of this happened in the space of ten minutes and as quickly as this outpouring had started, it stopped. Jackie felt terrible talking about this and left the session; I didn't hear from her for a month. In fact it wasn't Jackie I heard from next; it was John.

It Starts with Confusion

A vague feeling of confusion is commonly the first symptom of a relationship that is descending into a *narcissist-codependent* dynamic. The narcissist rarely unleashes his or her full pathology on their partner in one blast, revealing their flaws in small ways at first. This is a reason for one of the huge misconceptions around NPD, because the fully revealed personality disorder is so monstrous that those outside the relationship fail to understand the calculated escalation that turns seemingly strong, independent individuals into helpless shells. By the time the narcissist is out of the shadows, their partner has been worn into such a state of psychological exhaustion that they are unable to form the protective boundaries that are part and parcel of a normal healthy relationship.

Because the narcissist is such an expert at creating and maintaining an attractive self-image, they are often able to disarm their victims, following an episode of abuse, by a twin process of carefully apportioned blame: "If you hadn't made me look so bad in front of my friends I wouldn't have been so angry," and mock remorse: "I love you do much; I promise this will never happen again." The process works a treat on the codependent partner who accepts the poisoned chalice and redoubles their efforts to give the narcissist what they need. The increased attention serves to feed the narcissist but also to repulse them as they see their own projected neediness reflected back at them. As the unhealthy bond continues to develop and becomes embedded, verbal and physical abuse often escalates which inevitably leads to serious psychological and sometimes physical harm.

It was an extremely hot day and all of the windows were fully open. I was grateful for every breeze that came, for the room was sticky and the fan laboured to keep the air moving and the room comfortable enough for my patients and I to focus (the windows need to be closed during session because of the potential for people in the office next door to hear). I felt slightly irritable in the heat and was trying to calm myself when a call came through from John asking for my urgent help. He reported that he and Jackie had been attending a business dinner when Jackie seemed to start suffocating before yelling at him and leaving the restaurant. John found her outside and demanded she return and apologise. Instead Jackie ran away, literally ran as fast as she could, and did not return home until hours later. John was emphasising how Jackie needed help and that he was counting on me to help her as she was out of control and causing all sorts of issues for him. John also made reference to his faith in me to do a "good job" and to get Jackie back to her "normal" self.

He instructed me to call Jackie and arrange an appointment with her. I explained to him that it would be better if Jackie were to access me herself and acknowledge that she needs this help. He seemed irritated with this suggestion but Jackie did call.

Recognising the Signs of NPD

Here follows some of the warning signs commonly associated with narcissists:

- ! A lack of humility. Narcissists are 'never wrong' and never feel remorseful. Although they may apologise for a situation, this will almost always be accompanied by a thinly-disguised excuse with the victim blamed in some way.
- ! Since they believe they are never wrong, narcissists often react angrily when criticised.
- ! Narcissists are skilled at commanding the attention and admiration of others, often boasting about their achievements.
- ! Narcissists are so disconnected from themselves that they can't even begin to relate to others on an emotional level. Empathy and, by extension, love are alien concepts to them, although they are often able to put on an act to cover up this deficiency.
- ! Narcissists will often call and text their partner excessively; this controlling behaviour is often misconstrued as a sign of love and commitment.
- ! Narcissists without attention will become sulky, depressed or angry.
- ! Narcissists despise normality and see themselves as above everyday concerns (which rarely provide them with the special attention they crave).

This can mean they fail to hold down a job or handle finances responsibly, often deliberately engineering crises to direct attention on to them.

Please note here that there is a wealth of theory about, and numerous observations of, NPD behaviour. Not every box above needs to be ticked. NPD is more about an attitude and, although there is, of course, common ground shared by narcissists, they, like all humans, are individuals. Thus, there may be exceptions to the rule and even 'typical' narcissists may show more of one trait and less of another. Regardless, everyone with NPD governs, controls and feeds on their intimate partner, child or parent to survive.

The Perfect Partner

Ironically, one of the most common precursors to the *narcissist-codependent* relationship is the whirlwind romance that sweeps the victim off their feet. If a narcissist were to reveal their true nature at the outset of a relationship, they would quickly be tossed aside. Therefore they will work diligently to simulate the perfect partner, keeping up this charade for many weeks, or even months, before letting their real selves shine through.

Although romantic gestures should be appreciated and enjoyed, people must retain some healthy scepticism, particularly if they become aware of worrying inconsistencies in behaviour. Jackie's main recurring story is about how she does not understand what went wrong – or what she did wrong – because this was her dream relationship and everyone loves and admires John.

"I just don't understand what is wrong; no matter how hard I try I don't get it right," she told me.

One character trait that should ring alarm bells, even during the 'honeymoon period,' is a disproportionate reaction when the partner turns off the supply of attention.

Regardless of their romantic gestures and promises of love, the narcissist's real objectives are twofold: to feed directly off the admiration and appreciation the *codependent* lavishes on them, and to use that display of adoration, along with other aspect of their partner's appeal, to enhance their own image in the eyes of others.

As long as the attention is flowing their way, they will be an absolute delight and display all the charm and charisma they are capable of. But as soon as they feel they are 'losing the floor,' they are likely to rapidly change their demeanour, becoming withdrawn and sulky or irritable. Unlike a truly self-confident person, a narcissist will become agitated and sometimes quite unpleasant if their partner provides attention to their other friends, although they will do their best to hide these feelings at first.

Those with an instinct for self-preservation will often do a bit of subtle background research on a new romantic interest before becoming too committed. By talking to a narcissist's friends and family members they are more likely to uncover inconsistencies around career, status or history. Assessing their relationship with their parents, and previous romantic relationships, including how these ended, can throw up further insights, perhaps revealing a history of jealousy or violence. While nobody's background is perfect, if the person's track record suggests a very different character to the one they are outwardly showing, it is often best to get out early.

Another warning sign is selfish lovemaking, especially if there is a lot of aggression and/or perversion involved. This is why it is usually best not to rush into a sexual relationship before being sure that both people are caring and considerate of each other's needs.

Jackie: "Even sex hurts; I've told John many times that we need to get warmed up and do some nice things, like we did in the beginning, but now he just grabs me and it hurts. When I try to pull away he makes me pay for days with silence and by withdrawing from me."

No Capacity for Support

One of the most shocking realisations that often confirms a narcissist's lack of empathy is their response when their partner is having a bad time and is in need of support. As the narcissist is forced to give out attention they will immediately become sulky or resentful, blaming their partner for selfishly focusing on their needs. The narcissist is actually incapable of giving out genuine warmth despite their sophisticated ability to mock concern when around other people.

For others to assert their needs is a sign of rebellion to the narcissist who may punish them for their neediness, even if they are sick. This behaviour is cruelly dehumanising and eats away at the victim's being over time.

Seasons move so fast here in the UK. I have chosen Brighton, a wonderful seaside haven in southern England, and I am sitting here listening to the far off but loud cries of the seagulls as I complete the case insertions for this book.

Reflecting upon the kinds of behaviour displayed by someone with NPD towards a codependent, I find it difficult to put into words specific case examples. I've seen many codependents and helped them to unhook from their very unhealthy relationship dynamic; but there have been so many that it feels difficult to unravel them all.

However, this is probably mirroring what the codependent feels and experiences. In essence the narcissist chips, chips, chips away at their victim over time. The codependent knows that they have been destroyed but the main challenge is getting them to believe that the narcissist is being unreasonable and treating them unfairly.

Another challenge for the victim is to get them to give examples of the narcissist's cruelty without sounding guilty when doing so. Jackie, for example, would often retract her complaints about John because she felt guilty or unreasonable. After all, he "gives her so much," and, "is a really nice guy, if you knew him." Jackie oscillated between this very compassionate and loyal stance and a painful awakening about how John was and continued to be unreasonable.

Jackie's breakthrough came when she had an affair: "Michael, he is so affectionate; he touches my arm, looks at me when we are out and makes me feel really comfortable," she once said. "He keeps telling me to stop apologising. I am realising how starved I was, all those years gobbling up any crumb of thought, kindness and affection but it was ALL FAKE. Nothing felt like this! WHAT BROUGHT ME TO THE POINT OF FEELING I NEED TO APOLOGISE ALL THE TIME? JOHN NEVER ONCE APOLOGISED TO ME, NOT ONCE!

He's been charming and given me all the promises in the world but he was always patronising; WHY DID I NOT SEE THIS? NOTHING CHANGED! EVER!"

Jackie, by this time, was screaming and releasing pain and torment; yes, that's a good word for this: 'torment.' Jackie was almost howling whilst engaging with all of the wrongs that had befallen her.

All of the disappointments, punishments, unfairness, loneliness, hoping, anguish and PAIN. It was a PAIN she could not put into words. It was the release of a monstrous Hell she was finally realising she needed to separate from.

This was now a case of Jackie's survival – and I am not dramatising; it had got to a matter of life over death as Jackie had planned on taking her own life if she couldn't stop the pain.

The above is what I commonly describe as a 'shift' in my therapeutic work. Jackie had worked so very hard to get to this juncture where she was finally seeing the wood for the trees. She was realising that she had no power to change John; she was starting to accept that the hope she had held on to for year after painful year was without grounds. The situation she was – and had always been in – was hopeless and dangerous.

The Jekyll and Hyde Complex

NPD has a bipolar nature. The narcissist can be disarmingly pleasant and seemingly thoughtful at times, but when the weather changes other people hardly exist to them and probably wouldn't even want to be in the same room for fear of being verbally or even physically attacked.

This can be understood when one realises that the narcissist's default state is one of emptiness. When supplied with attention from the outside world, they are satisfied, albeit temporarily, and can be good-natured to those around them. Once the supply is gone and their reserves are depleted, the negative feelings resurface, the mood crashes and the *codependent* finds themselves walking on eggshells again.

The conversation between myself, John and Jackie continued as follows:

John: "Please take care of Jackie, Michael, she is not her normal self. She's becoming unbearable and behaving in really abnormal ways."

Jackie: "I cannot walk on eggshells anymore; I try to please him but what's the point? I cannot do it anymore. When he walks in front of me he gets my hand and pulls me along because I'm not walking fast enough; I want him to hold my hand with affection, not control.

"I couldn't help it, Michael. I just broke free and ran and ran and ran. I felt that I was suffocating; I couldn't get my breath. I felt that if I didn't run...I don't know what. I ran for what seemed hours; I don't think John even ran after me, I didn't look back to check. In fact, all I remember is breaking free and running; running just to get away. I was gone for several hours. I sat on a park bench and just stared into space. Eventually I got cold and had nowhere else to go so I went home. That's really the time John demanded I sort myself out, saying that it was outrageous me leaving him in the street like that and asking if I didn't know how much he worried about me when I was gone?"

Disowned Feelings and Projection

The person with NPD has none of their own reserves on which to draw if they feel unfulfilled; but, totally out of touch with their feelings, they will rarely admit that they feel 'down.'

To tarnish their fake self-image with the impurity of vulnerability is unacceptable so they will instead start blaming those around them for making them act in certain ways. Once again we see the hallmark of the domestic abuse perpetrator who blames the victim for 'making' them lash out due to some arbitrary departure from required behaviour. But as there is no real correlation between the victim's behaviour and the perpetrator's abuse, the victim is reduced to a state of hyper-vigilance that will eventually harm both the mind and body.

Worse still, the narcissist disowns all that they despise about themselves and, through the psychological mechanism of projection, sees their inner sense of worthlessness and disgust personified in their victim. The *codependent* then becomes 'fair game' for any and all verbal or physical 'acting out' – an object into which the narcissist pours all of their repressed rage and hatred.

I had a couples session with John and Jackie quite far, probably about 14 months, into our work together. Jackie had asked to bring John in to clarify some boundary settings she felt she needed in order to continue living with him. In the session we discussed Jackie's 'running.' Her tearing away from John and running was becoming a regular occurrence, at least twice each month.

The specific situation we focused upon was the situation at the supermarket described earlier in this book. Jackie was trying to set a boundary with John whereby he hears what she says and respects her so I set the boundary that Jackie was not to interrupt John describing the events that lead up to her 'running' and that, in turn, I would request the same of John and that he would hear and be quiet during Jackie's recollection of events.

John: "We were at the supermarket checkout after a long day of Christmas shopping.

There was a long queue and the weather was bad. I had bought a two-for-one offer and the receipt was wrong. The checkout girl argued with me that my voucher had expired and she couldn't do anything about it. She was disrespectful and rude. I told her again, in a kind way, that I was a regular customer and the voucher was only out by a day. Then people behind started to mutter and criticise because we were holding them up. It was terrible; I will never shop with them again. So, I started to pack the bags in a hurry. Next thing I know Jackie is crying and taking off – running away."

Jackie: "Yes, the voucher had expired. I had explained this to him earlier and he had told me that since he was a regular customer it would be OK and to not be stupid. At the checkout John was trying to convince the checkout girl that she could overlook just one day. He was swoozing her. When she stuck to her guns and the people behind started to get restless, John got angry and starting packing things in bags carelessly. I explained that we would need to be careful as there were some fragile Christmas gifts I had bought earlier in some of the bags. John just gave me a warning look and continued to shove the shopping in without any consideration. I could see and hear that things were being smashed and broken. I – just – I – I – couldn't breathe, I felt invisible, I felt scared, I felt deflated, hopeless – I had to run!"

John, Jackie and I discussed this event at some length. John was becoming more and more agitated as he attempted to have me side with him and see his point of view and to agree how 'silly' and unreasonable Jackie was.

I asked John if it was acceptable to seemingly ignore Jackie and break her things, to put a queue of people being frustrated before Jackie's pleading. He eventually conceded this one point but then said to me: "So you've solved this one incident. What about all the thousands of others Jackie keeps going on about.

"What can we do about those? How are you going to fix all of these other problems Jackie has?" I responded that it might need a slight change of attitude on his part and to consider some boundaries – or a safe word such as 'lampshade': we could say 'lampshade' when Jackie does not feel heard or feels threatened.

Shockingly, but expected all the same, John's guns turned on me. He exploded and accused me of being a fake, saying that he was "tired of my advertisement to get more money from him," and that Jackie was, "done with this stupid nonsense," and that I was, "hurting rather than helping her." He told me that he would take me to court and sue me for every penny he had paid for Jackie – plus all damages."

In our next individual session, Jackie told me how pleased she was that John had shown his 'other side.' "My friends and even family feel I'm making things up or exaggerating," she said. "John is such a charming and successful man. No one believes me; no one gets how it is and when I try to explain it and the words come out of my mouth it sounds ridiculous, even to me. I sound like I am so ungrateful."

When there is no source of attention, the narcissist makes it their obsession to find one. Although they can get a certain amount from the world at large, they still need a constant supply at home to ensure they don't have to spend time alone with themselves. The pursuit of a love partner becomes an obsession and the traits they look for are on the one hand attractiveness and status, as this enhances their own image, and, on the other, a poor boundary function. This will give them the purchase they need to gradually take control of the relationship – and wear down the partner's own identity.

Jackie, we must remember, is a very accomplished person in the academic world. John is very successful in the scientific world. Jackie's most common phrase is: "I just don't understand. When we are out, John shows me off (Jackie is also stunningly attractive and very well-presented) but when we are alone it's as if I don't exist; I'm invisible. I am not like this in any other part of my world and with any other relationships, only when I'm with John. My friends and family and colleagues are great and I am liked. I just don't understand."

The Child in an Adult's Body

The narcissist is like an angry child who has never grown up. As explained earlier, they can emerge from families in which there was a profound lack of nurture or, conversely, those in which they were very much doted upon and 'spoilt.'

The narcissist's emotional development is arrested at around the years of five to seven and they never develop the moderating, objective part of the mind that weighs up actions and effects; this makes them exceedingly impulsive and sometimes aggressive.

Just like a child, the narcissist only really understands their own emotional pain and that becomes justification enough for any of their own actions. They are intensely ego-driven and feel entitled to preferential treatment, demanding instant gratification and unable to accept being denied what they want, when they want it.

The narcissist is the archetypal con-artist and has no respect for the boundaries of others.

They are often highly intelligent and always possessed of dangerous street cunning, adept at hiding their true nature and using their acute perception and skills of analysis to select the best tactic to appeal to the emotions of their victim. In fact, the high level narcissist is supremely intuitive and manipulative, able to accurately assess weakness, rapidly move themselves into a position of trust and to begin to gather intelligence and elicit closely-guarded secrets – all used to strengthen their position. Once accepted as a trusted partner, the narcissist lives a parasitic existence, taking what they can from their host with no consideration of the effects. This includes money, sex and less tangible resources such as their victim's mental focus and emotional energy.

However, no matter how much is given and how often, the narcissist can never be fulfilled and will always need more.

Jackie is consistently exhausted and feels ground down, depleted, worthless and hopeless.

Narcissists are sometimes divided into somatic and cerebral subtypes, with the somatic narcissist requiring more of the physical and sensory supply (e.g. sex and the power that money brings) and the cerebral narcissist more intent on lapping up attention and recognition for their intelligence and abilities.

John's most common utterance was: "I don't feel respected. Do you know who I am?"

In a narcissist's world, all interaction is a competition where there can be only one winner; what's more, they believe other people think in the same way.

But just as in the myth of the vampire, the narcissist has to be allowed into their victim's private space before they can begin to suck them dry.

The narcissist knows that material wealth is a powerful source of attraction, and they will work diligently to create an illusion of power and self-sufficiency. On the surface they may display and talk about their possessions and exalted lifestyle: prestigious career, high-value homes, expensive cars, fine clothes, exotic holidays and the like. But delve beneath the surface and all is rarely what it seems.

The narcissist's sense of entitlement together with loose morals, a lack of accountability and a disdain for 'normality' will often lead them to take shortcuts and risks, and to obtain wealth by deception, the profligate use of credit and, of course, by taking advantage of the generosity of others whenever possible.

As mentioned throughout, John is very wealthy – in the millions. Has he achieved his wealth fairly – if there is such a thing? Maybe not. But while most narcissists do exaggerate and create a false image of accomplishment and wealth, their circumstances are diverse and it is important to understand that someone with genuine accumulated wealth can still be a narcissist – and they will use their position of wealth as a tool for self-nurturing.

The narcissist will begrudgingly do the minimum expected to fulfil their responsibilities to the 'system' while creating problems and crises around them. The true extent of the chaos in which they exist usually only becomes apparent after they have formed a powerful bond with their codependent victim.

Any attempt to expose the real situation is keenly felt as a wound to their self-esteem and the narcissist will react in the customary fashion: rage, denial and blame – followed by a need to boost their narcissistic supply.

Attempting to expose their hidden shame is futile; the narcissist isn't emotionally developed enough to consciously accept and process this emotion.

The Green-eyed Monster

The narcissist is characterised by intense jealousy, based on insecurity, and are sometimes aroused by sexual perversions. In heterosexual relationships, there is often a simultaneous obsession and hatred towards the opposite sex which comes out verbally and physically when conflicts arise. In fact, the narcissist will often use gender-specific slurs as they attempt to run their victim's self-esteem into the ground.

The narcissist has never learned that a relationship has to be based on trust and honesty to flourish and will constantly lie and use dishonest tactics to gain control. Honesty is equated with vulnerability and weakness, attributes the narcissist will go to any ends to deny in themselves. The narcissist is so skilled in the art of manipulation, and so lacking in real self-awareness, that they can start to believe their own lies.

Codependency and Hyper-vigilance

One of the most stressful and damaging effects of being in a relationship with a narcissist is the constant state of hyper-vigilance needed to avoid trauma. The victim is constantly in a heightened state of threat-detection, always ready to react to the next outburst or attack.

The problem is that the narcissist's mood is unpredictable and connected with their own warped inner reality rather than external circumstances. This leaves the victim perpetually in a state of uncertainty, never able to fully relax.

In the field of behavioural psychology, hyper-vigilance has been observed in rats.

When rewards are consistently accompanied by a green light, rats will display relaxed behaviour, but when these two events are disconnected (i.e. the rewards are given at random), the rats display repetitive, compulsive behaviour.

Running, running, running. Jackie's 'running' is a behaviour related to high anxiety in a stressed environment. When we experience extreme levels of anxiety, our body reverts back to what was needed to survive prior to our 21st century civilisation. Before our modern world we largely became stressed because there was a physical threat to us from competitive villagers or animals. When faced with such imminent threat we either 'fight' our way out of it or we choose 'flight' and run for the hills. This is commonly known as the 'fight or flight mechanism.' Jackie's running is her way of managing the threat and escaping from it, thereby reducing her anxiety to a more manageable level.

Interestingly, because we run and fight better with an empty stomach and bladder, under extreme stress it's usual for us to vomit and/or experience diarrhoea. Jackie has been suffering with symptoms that are modernly known as IBS (Irritable Bowel Syndrome) which is often associated with stress.

The toxic effects of hyper-vigilance on the body and brain should not be underestimated as large amounts of 'stress chemicals,' for example cortisone, have been shown to damage brain tissue. The *codependent* in a relationship with a narcissist may become steadily more confused and their thinking increasingly deranged until total breakdown occurs.

The effects can be magnified by a cruel psychological process known as 'gaslighting'.

This is where the narcissist deliberately sets out to loosen the victim's grip on reality by tampering with their environment and manipulating events. For example, they might move their victim's car keys to convince them they have mislaid them or pretend a conversation progressed differently to the way the victim remembered it, even enlisting the help of allies to back up their version of events. The more 'unsure' of their own mind the *codependent* becomes, the more control the narcissist can take.

Other tricks favoured by the narcissist include constantly switching their preferences so that the *codependent* can never make the right choice, and steadfastly refusing to carry out the most basic of their expected duties giving the *codependent* an uneven share of domestic work, grinding them down further.

Jackie works in a demanding full-time job and carries out all duties in the home. All of them. John never even clears the table after dinner or helps to load the dishwasher! When Jackie would complain about this John would tell her to stop being so 'needy.'

Eventually the *codependent*, broken of all means of rebellion, may start to display symptoms of a phenomenon known as Stockholm Complex or 'capture-bonding.' They become sympathetic with their abuser, taking on their opinions and blaming themselves for their situation.

In essence, they become the perfect projection of what the narcissist hates about him or herself. This can lead to an intensification of the abuse. This is probably the main reason why victims find it difficult to leave or unhook from their NPD partner. They become so lost, so out of the loop of their own reality.

The Death of the Narcissist

The life of a narcissist is tragic, but the way in which they can and will drag anyone they bond with into their nightmare means that sympathy is a very risky attitude to take. To the narcissist, sympathy is just another form of attention, and they will gladly lap it up until their victims have no more to give.

Underneath the mask lives a frightened and angry child, afraid of being abandoned and ignored and desperate to replace those feelings with the drugs of physical pleasure, admiration and attention. Other people exist solely to gratify these needs and are, in their eyes, objects with no right to their own feelings or motivations.

Sadly, as the narcissist begins to age, they lose some of their physical appeal while, at the same time, their history of cruelty and dishonesty begins to catch up with them. They may end up profoundly alone and destroyed by debt, with nowhere left to go to escape from the inner darkness they have been running from for so long.

PART 2: UNHOOKING & RECOVERING FROM A NARCISSIST

5. BREAKING THE DYNAMIC: HOW DO I QUIT YOU?

"At first I was afraid, I was petrified. Kept Thinking I could never live without you by my side." -
I Will Survive (performed by Gloria Gaynor; written by Freddie Perren/Dino Fekkaris)

Co-dependency, Addiction and Self-Loathing

Co-dependency can be partly understood as a disease of self-loathing. By focusing all of their being on serving other people, co-dependents deny themselves the full light of awareness and try to nourish themselves from the reflected light of other people's appreciation and gratitude. But the presence of self-hate, lurking in the background, leads to a constant, gnawing self-doubt. They sometimes see their own self-disgust lurking behind the smiles of those they are attempting to please and they obsessively work harder to be a better partner, employee, child or parent.

This attachment to another person is an addiction every bit as damaging as an attachment to a substance or behaviour – in fact it can be more so, since the narcissist actively works to become a more irresistible fix.

I worked in drug dependency units for many years, and working with someone that is codependent and unhooking them from a toxic relationship is ten times more difficult and stressful than helping someone off a highly addictive drug. I'm sure that anyone who works with a similar population will scream 'yes,' in agreement with this statement.

The very same mechanism that is at work in a substance abuser lurks within a codependent, It is the voice that convinces the self that,'it will be OK,''why change?,''oh, just one more last one,''it's not that bad,''no-one knows them like I do,' etc.

What is worse for a codependent is that when they explode, scream for recognition, run away or plead they are reinforcing their own fears of inadequacy and the thoughts and beliefs they hold about being a bad person. The hole they dig for themselves in this unhealthy addiction is so deep that no one can convince them until they themselves have had a glimpse that this is not working. This can be after years of being hooked or within the first few months or weeks

Yes, it is possible for a codependent to be hooked within weeks: the extreme charm, praise and adoration shown by the narcissist – the dance that coaches and reels them in – is so real it seems to be exactly the fix the codependent needs in their life. The toxic feeling that, 'everything is good in my life now,' and that, 'this was the moment he or she arrived to fix it all,' is so strong and overwhelmingly 'right' that the codependent strives to recreate that 'hit' throughout their upcoming battle with neglect, invisibility, abuse and degradation.

Addiction and the DSM-5

Co-dependency is not, at this time, officially recognised as an addiction, but that does not mean that we can't look to the DSM-5 for information and guidance. It must be realised that diagnoses in psychiatry are permanently in a state of debate and new editions of the DSM will reflect current academic opinion.

For example, the DSM-5 has eradicated separate substance abuse and dependency diagnoses and adopted an addiction scale that runs from mild to severe, explaining the decision as follows:

"In DSM-IV, the distinction between abuse and dependence was based on the concept of abuse as a mild or early phase and dependence as the more severe manifestation. In practice, the abuse criteria were sometimes quite severe. The revised substance use disorder, a single diagnosis, will better match the symptoms that patients experience."

At the same time, the manual casts its net wider and now includes gambling, with internet gaming added to Section III with the following caveat:

"Disorders listed there require further research before their consideration as formal disorders. This condition is included to reflect the scientific literature on persistent and recurrent use of Internet games, and a preoccupation with them, can result in clinically significant impairment or distress."

Perhaps, in time, *co-dependency* will be brought into the fold but, in the meantime, co-dependents and therapists who work with them can derive much benefit from the models of addiction used to understand and help those addicted to substances.

It has also become very clear to me, from working at the chalkface of therapy, that there are certain patterns that emerge time after time, but that whenever I work with someone new I never know how that is going to unfold. What they bring to me at times is so masked, so hidden under layers and layers of co-habiting themes and stories that there is usually a waiting game to play before I can begin to formulate what happened to this person and how we are going to help them out of this stuckness.

As I get into the fourth, fifth or eighth meeting (each person requiring a slightly different length of time before they feel safe and connected enough to dig with me) with a codependent (not forgetting that the original issues they come in with are not about 'being' a codependent but about the symptoms that stem from being a codependent within the claws of a narcissist) the pattern begins to emerge. It may be slightly different in terms of their story, their demographic or their position in the relationship but it raises its face. However, I do think, 'hmm, let's not be hasty as it may be something I am looking for but that isn't really there.

So my role at this stage is to check out 'stuff.' Yes, I call it stuff: I approach all of this cloudy, confusing, scary space with a patient while remaining open enough to see themes develop that can help with our understanding of the root: the core elements of their issues or – in a nutshell – what is really going on for them and how they got to be in the chair opposite me.

This is the moment when I ask some big questions; questions you reading this book may need to ask yourself or a dear one; questions like:

'You said that was a deal-breaker yet you're still in the same situation – what keeps you there?'

'It is fear that usually keeps us stuck. What does fear look like to you? What are you fearful of?'

'What is reality and what is hope for you? How long have things been good, and how long have you been in love with what could be?'

'Have you been in this place before and who with? How did you survive that ending?'

'What are your thoughts about meeting someone healthy for you in the future?'

Exploring these and similar questions will bring to the surface oxymorons, polemic states of being and areas of conflict that usually turn on a big, bright light of recognition for those waist high in an NPD/codependency relationship.

It is worth spending some time considering one factor on which escaping from any form of addiction hinges: motivation.

The Role of Motivation

Motivation is not a quality you either have or don't have: some people claim they 'have no motivation,' when the reality is that they are motivated – just not enough to put in the effort that's required to change.

So motivation can be assessed by degree (how much motivation there is) and type (what the source of the motivation is). For example, a co-dependent may become aware that their submissive behaviour is setting a poor example to their children and that may be the strongest source of their motivation to change. Alternatively, they may have a strong desire to follow a particular career path and realise that their relationship is holding them back from putting the necessary effort into that goal.

And unfortunately, in difficult circumstances, that motivation can be staying alive and not killing oneself, or curtailing the murder of the narcissist. The 'stuckness' felt by codependents in an NPD relationship can become so hopeless that these extremes are not that uncommon. However, when such deaths do occur, they are reported as 'completed suicide' or 'provoked murder' and rarely is the motivation examined. A much-needed area of research would involve looking at the relationship dynamic and family history of those involved; this could raise awareness and increase focus on the therapeutic and prevention level.

When co-dependents and therapists understand that motivation is a pliable quality, it provides something to work with. In other words, various therapeutic techniques can be applied to increase the degree of motivation until it is strong enough to effect real change.

The most basic but also the most powerful of these therapeutic tools is to 'mirror' the client. Through accurate mirroring, much awareness can be elicited which forms the start of the motivation to change. Take this example:

'So he did this last year, you told him that you were worth more than that, and after he did this again last month you are still with him. So you are worth more and still with him?'

Or:

'It has been three years since you held hands or had intimacy and she has continued having affairs. You have compensated by drinking more every night and this works for you?'

Accurate and honest reflecting needs to be carried out in a trusting relationship and my clients need to have reached the position where they feel that what I say, no matter how hard it is for them to hear it, is for their good and delivered in a caring and compassionate way. Therapists working in this way visibly see the light bulbs go on when they get this reflection right and use it at the right time.

It really depends at what stage of development the person is at: it is usual for codependents to go in and out of therapy many times before they get to the stage where they are ready to fully consider the possibility of leaving or changing up their relationship. This is much the same as a person who is dependent on substances, such as alcohol or drugs, as it can take them several attempts before they are physically and emotionally ready. At times accurate reflection can be too challenging and the client will feel that I do not understand them, or they will feel guilty talking about their partner in such a way. However, every exposure to friends, family, strangers (witnessing uncomfortable interaction or treatment), self realisation and last, but not least, their therapist chipping away with "this relationship dynamic really does not seem to be good for you," is all part of that necessary withdrawal process that has to be achieved before the patient can lock in the motivators that will provide them with the strength to protect their sense of self from the harmful contraindications of this toxic and unhealthy love nest.

So, before motivation must come awareness. Whether a co-dependent is trying to help themselves under their own steam or with the help of a therapist, there has to be the recognition that there is a problem and the desire to change. Otherwise there is only a token effort and the entrenched pattern of behaviour will simply keep on repeating itself; as Einstein once put it:

"Insanity (is) doing the same thing over and over again and expecting different results."

So motivation has to be preceded by awareness of either the harmful effects of the addictive behaviour or the benefits of breaking free – preferably both. This is the starting point of the 'Stages of Change' model that follows:

Stages of Change

There are several models of addiction which the co-dependent and therapist can draw inspiration from, but one of the most popular and effective is the Stages of Change Model devised by Professors James Prochaska and Carlo DiClemente in the 1970s. Also referred to as the TTM (Transtheoretical Model), this breaks down the process of addiction recovery into six parts.

1. Pre-contemplation
At the pre-contemplation stage, any recognition of a need to change is mostly unconscious. There may be the occasional flash of awareness, when the relationship and health costs of addiction are recognised, but at this stage the benefits provided by the object of addiction, whether a substance, activity or person, outweighs those costs. In the example of codependency, the security and validity gained from the relationship seem worth the pain. The defining feature of Stage One of the TTM model is the lack of any real motivation to change.

Moreover, it is very rare for someone to access my services at this stage unless they are pushed by a dear one to access help.

Even if pushed and sitting with me due to the encouragement of a loved one, nothing, nothing will change until the co-dependent is ready and, as mentioned before, this can take several attempts, sometimes over several years, before full engagement is made and we can investigate change. Even then, at this determined stage, the fear of change will be immense and present an enormous challenge. It is a particularly difficult stage for all concerned as there is hope and then no hope; more pain; more affirmation that they cannot survive without their narcissist and fear of being alone forever (for who could want them) etc.

I usually bring the serenity prayer into this part of the work. It is important to help the person know that they cannot change their narcissist, they can only change themselves, and that until this wisdom sets in they will continue taking care of their narcissist's requirements, needs and wants, feeding them at the expense of themselves in the hope that they will get more of the good, intimate, adoring, charming crumbs of affection, recognition and respect.

2. Contemplation

When the desire to break free of addiction emerges, the person has moved on to Stage Two of the TTM. This is an exploratory phase and there may be little motivation to actually put in the work necessary. The person may lack confidence in their ability to beat their addiction, may waver in their commitment and may think and talk in terms of taking action in 'the future.' However, they are at least aware of the need to change and open to thinking about the issue.

This part of the process is a fragile one, and the person may slip back into Stage One at any time. To move on to Stage Three, they have to reach a point where they accept that the negative effects of their addiction outweigh the benefits. They then have to make that crucial decision to commit to the process of becoming unhooked.

3. Preparation

Having risen to the challenge and accepted responsibility for the change process, the person is now in a position to weigh up their options and decide on a strategy. They might decide to book into a rehab centre or seek a therapist (if they are not already working with one), or they may even feel able to handle the journey themselves. Their confidence and commitment levels are likely to be high at this point as they anticipate the benefits of freedom. The quicker they can take action the more likely they are to make some real progress because, despite their decision to change, it is still possible for them to slip back into the contemplation stage at any time.

4. Action

Change is finally occurring at Stage Four with the person learning new skills and drawing deeper insights about their behaviour along the way. The initial period of action is characterised by enthusiasm as the recovering addict discards old ways of behaving and embraces change. If this early momentum can be sustained for six months, the person has reached the Maintenance stage.

5. Maintenance

By Stage Five, a lot of progress will have been made. The person is not free of their addiction but they have established positive patterns of behaviour, gained more self-control and become aware of high risk situations.

For co-dependents, this will involve being conscious of when their narcissistic partner is pushing their buttons and stimulating their need to please.

The next task for the recovering addict is to bring together what they have learned and integrate their new way of being into their lives. Although their addiction is now largely under control, they do need to remain vigilant as relapse is still a risk.

6. Termination

The person has now successfully created a new self-image which is no longer defined by the substance – or person – they were once addicted to. Their new, healthier behaviour patterns have become fully integrated in their lives and they are reaping the benefits. The presence of the addictive substance, situation or person no longer tempts them from the path.

Even in this final stage of the TTM, there is a small chance of relapse, perhaps in the event of a significant downturn in circumstances, but that risk is now very low.

In substance abuse, embarking on the road to recovery requires that the drugs or drink are removed from the picture. When the object of addiction is a person, the blunt truth is that there has to be a separation for full recovery to happen. Unlike substances, addictive people can change their behaviour to maintain their grip on the addict. For example, what is more compelling to the co-dependent than the phrase, "But I need you; I can't live without you."

Getting Out is the Only Path to Healing?

The prognosis for someone suffering with NPD is extremely poor although there are professionals who profess to have had an element of success using various types of therapy. The extent of that element would be interesting to study. There is such a shortage of research in this field and it is this that perpetuates the suffering of those silent *codependents*. However, positive outcomes are very unlikely since narcissists, by their very nature, usually refuse to accept there is anything wrong with them, and those that do attend therapy tend to leave early on in the process, often believing the therapist to be 'beneath them'.

In my 21 years of practice, no narcissist has ever engaged and worked through therapy with me; instead, they tend to use the language learned during their short time in therapy against their partner and even against me. They engage with therapy up to the point of being challenged. Then it is just too much to question their fragile façade any further. Narcissists only usually show up in rooms because their victims invite them in the hope of change. Attitude is a very difficult phenomenon to adjust when the person is unwilling, or so scared, they are unable to try.

However, there is hope for the *codependents* who have escaped a narcissist's clutches – but only if they get out. There are no two ways about it: a narcissist's victim cannot heal if they remain part of the toxic dynamic in the same way as a wound will not heal around a foreign object.

As soon as the *codependent* begins to assert their own existence within the relationship, the narcissist will immediately step up their efforts to quell the rebellion – and they will win.

Having read this far, you may be convinced that your partner, work colleague, parent or adult child are narcissistic or you may still have your doubts. If you are reading this because you are concerned about a significant other suffering from being in a relationship with a narcissist then it is very important that you tread carefully. An NPD is expertly skilled at isolating their victim so if the narcissistic man, woman or transexual gets wind that you are 'interfering' chances are that they will spin a web that separates you from them too.

Whether you identify as a codependent or not, understand that behaviours that attempt to humiliate, isolate, control or abuse are unacceptable, and the sooner you stand up to your abuser and seek help, the shorter your road to healing and happiness will be. As always, you are only able to change your own attitudes and behaviour, and you will soon realise whether those efforts are rewarded with the respect they deserve or are incompatible with your relationship.

For those who have been living as a codependent for their entire lives, having the spotlight turned on them and their needs can be uncomfortable and even overwhelming at first. Without somebody to serve and provide for, the emptiness and insecurity inside becomes revealed. For support, they should seek help, read a lot and talk online with other victims.

If you do seek to work with a therapist, you should make certain that the professional you choose has a proven background in relationship work. It is a tough job holding a person that is very damaged and carefully but purposefully peeling back each layer of the abuse to reveal the victim's true self. This type of systemic work will aid you in seeing the bigger picture by helping you to understand the system you were working within, the dynamics at play and your own journey thus far. Codependency's worst characteristic is that of too much tolerance for the other and not enough for the self. You can work on how to stop blaming yourself for everything and on identifying and respecting your own needs as you move slowly along the path to healing.

Being trained by your narcissist that you are the 'problem' and you are 'wrong' takes a lot of undoing. If you have left a narcissistic spouse or romantic partner behind there is also a grieving process to go through, and work to be done to ensure previous patterns of relating are not repeated, either with a previous partner or someone else.

AFTERWORD

NPD and CD are not pretty subjects to write about. However, I hope that this book will bring relief to anyone experiencing this type of relationship. The greatest reward in doing my job is to see the relief in a person's face when they learn, understand and 'get' that they are NOT alone; NPD is a real issue and it is more common than people think.

The four major tasks in hand for a complete and lasting recovery are: understanding the true definition of dignity; healthy tolerance for self and others; serenity and healthy compassion for self and others.

Codependents, I have discovered, are missing a template on how to be with an intimate other, usually stemming from chaos when growing up or not being taught that it is OK for boundaries regarding self and other to exist.

After many, many years in academia and working at the chalkface of therapy, I've learnt so much from all the brave and engaging people I have met. I considered joining a research team or going back into teaching. But with my family and friends scattered, and with the intensive work I do visiting people in my rooms in London, Devon and Miami, not to mention over Skype™, I felt that to restrict myself to a faculty would hinder my continuing with my chosen path: working with those that desperately want and need change.

So after much deliberation, and working with my own psychologist in session after session, I decided to write a series of books - *"At the Chalkface of Therapy"* - about common issues brought to therapy, balancing evidenced facts about these issues with real examples of how people have worked through them to create a better life.

I have a lot of people that have worked with me to be thankful to. If it were not for all their hard work and input and wisdom I would never have been able to write this for you and your dear ones.

Remember this: if you are thinking of leaving a narcissist then plan carefully and choose the timing to be safe and manageable.

Jackie is living with John. She decided that the wealth and the opportunity that their lifestyle brings was too much to leave. She continues to work with me; John continues to pay. Jackie no longer does her 'running' and, as a coping strategy, she has focused more on her work and, of course, on herself by dropping into me. It is not my job to make decisions for people I see. I do not condone violence and I hold the hope that eventually people like Jackie will reach a more peaceful and more manageable place. Life is a journey; it can take weeks, months and even years for a CD to unhook from a narcissist. I guess it is all down to choice and timing.

LINKS & FURTHER INFORMATION

To find out more about Michael Acton-Coles or to contact him please visit the Acton-Coles Counselling & Psychology website:

www.acclinics.com

To go straight to Michael's articles and blog page, please go to:

www.acclinics.com/articles

You will be able to filter articles by category on the right-hand side of that page. If there are any articles you find particularly interesting or useful I would appreciate your comments and your help in circulating them by using the social media sharing tools below each article. You can also interact with me in the following ways:

Facebook: www.facebook.com/acclinicsUK
Twitter: www.twitter.com/acclinics
LinkedIn: www.linkedin.com/pub/michael-acton-coles/2b/556/104

For further information on relationship issues, co-dependency and addictions, the following organisations (continued overleaf) may be useful:

Alcoholics Anonymous
www.alcoholics-anonymous.org.uk

Al-Anon
www.al-anonuk.org.uk

Co-Dependents Anonymous (CoDA)
www.coda-uk.org

Relate
https://www.relate.org.uk

Finally, if you have any constructive feedback on this book or any personal experiences with narcissism and/or codependency that you would like to share, please contact me via email:

office@acclinics.com

GLOSSARY OF TERMS

American Psychiatric Association (APA): The largest professional association of psychiatrists and trainee psychiatrists in the world. The APA publish the *Diagnostic and Statistic Manual of Mental Disorders*.

Antisocial Personality Disorder (ASPD): A personality disorder characterised by a lack of respect for the rights of others, often involving acts of aggression and violence.

Bipolar: In psychiatry, bipolar refers to a disorder that causes fluctuation in mood between mania and depression.

Borderline Personality Disorder (BPD): A personality disorder characterised by extreme emotional instability and impulsive behaviour, including self-harm.

Cerebral narcissist: A narcissistic subtype where attention is manipulated largely by non-physical attributes such as intelligence and status.

Cluster B disorders: A grouping of personality disorders within the DSM-5, known as the 'Dramatic, emotional, erratic disorders.'

Codependency (CD): A feature of a relationship whereby one partner enables another's addiction or poor mental health.

Domestic Abuse: A pattern of behaviour which involves one member of a domestic relationship abusing another whether physically, emotionally, sexually or in other ways.

DSM-5: The latest (2013) edition of the *Diagnostic and Statistic Manual of Mental Disorders*. Published by the APA, it standardises and classifies mental disorders.

False ego: A false self or mask created to hide one's own insecurities.

Gaslighting: A psychological strategy used by abusers to manipulate the reality of their victims.

Grandiosity: An inflated sense of self-importance; one of the distinguishing features of NPD.

Histrionic Personality Disorder (HPD): A personality disorder characterised by attention-seeking behaviour, often through inappropriate sexual activity and exaggerated emotions.

Narcissistic Personality Disorder (NPD): A personality disorder characterised by self-obsession, an inflated sense of importance and a need for admiration.

Narcissistic rage: A display of extreme anger as a reaction to a perceived injury to a person's self-esteem.

Narcissistic supply: A source of admiration or positive attention.

Obsessive-compulsive disorder (OCD): An anxiety disorder characterised by repetitive behaviours.

Passive Dependent Personality: A psychoanalytic term for the personality type likely to become the victim in a *narcissist-codependent* relationship.

Pathology: The study of disease.

Personality disorder: A category of mental disorders characterised by maladaptive behaviours and negative inner experiences.

Psyche: The totality of the mind (conscious and unconscious); the subject of psychological study.

Somatic narcissist: A narcissistic subtype where attention is manipulated largely by physical attributes such as sex and physical pleasure.

Symptomatology: The combined symptoms of a disease.

Trait: A quality or characteristic.